# Risk Management

## Second edition

College of Occupational Therapists

College of
Occupational
Therapists

**This edition published in 2010**
by the College of Occupational Therapists
106–114 Borough High Street
London SE1 1LB
www.COT.org.uk

First published in Great Britain in 2006 by the College of Occupational Therapists

**Author:** Henny Pearmain on behalf of the College of Occupational Therapists
**Category:** Guidance

Other enquiries about this document should be addressed to the Practice department at the above address.

*British Library Cataloguing in Public Data*
A catalogue record for this book is available from the British Library.

While every effort has been made to ensure accuracy, the College of Occupational Therapists shall not be liable for any loss or damage either directly or indirectly resulting from the use of this publication.

ISBN 978-1-905944-24-8

Typeset by Servis Filmsetting Ltd, Stockport, Cheshire
Digitally printed on demand in Great Britain by the Lavenham Press, Suffolk

**Mixed Sources**
Product group from well-managed
forests and other controlled sources
www.fsc.org Cert no. SA-COC-1565
© 1996 Forest Stewardship Council
FSC

# Contents

# 1   Introduction

## What is risk management?

This guidance document will enable you to be aware of the requirements and responsibilities that you have in the area of risk and its management. Given the growing variety of occupational therapy settings, it can provide only a broad understanding of the principles of risk assessment and management, but it will also identify a number of other information resources currently available. It aims to provide guidance that is relevant and useful to practitioners across the UK, although you need to be aware of your local and country's policies. You should be aware that manual handling is covered in detail in a separate specific guidance document (COT 2006a).

Risk management is an intrinsic part of governance, service user safety and the provision of a quality care service. It is written into national standards for health, social care and education across the UK. Risk assessment and its management are not optional extras for you, but should be an inherent part of your safe and effective everyday practice. All service providers should have a set of policies and procedures in place relating to the management of risk.

In most environments risk management is seen as the employer or worker looking at the risks that arise in the workplace and then putting sensible health and safety measures in place to control them. For you, as an occupational therapy practitioner, risk management should be a broader concept. Risk-taking can have positive potential for individuals and their carers/families. People frequently take risks with the expectation and hope of gaining a beneficial outcome, for example learning to drive. For this reason, risk management should involve assessing and managing any kind of incident, event or 'hazard' that might cause harm, but managing it so that the potential benefit is gained and any likelihood of harm is adequately reduced. The relationship between you and the service user is key to effective risk management. 'Users should be seen as equal partners in the process and outcomes of risk assessment and management' (Barry 2007). This process can guide care decisions, enabling service users to take positive risks in a safe and appropriate way.

The principles remain the same whether the potential harm or benefit is to people, buildings or organisations. When asked, most people consider risk management to include actions to prevent injury or harm from physical hazards such as chemicals or equipment, or even perhaps from other people. However, you need to give broader consideration to procedures and systems in the workplace, along with activities such as communication and team-working.

For the purpose of this document a hazard is anything that has the potential to cause harm in any way. Risk is the possibility or likelihood, at any level, that this may occur, together with a measure of the effect. Positive risks are those that have the opportunity for benefit or gain if well managed.

Risk assessment is the first stage in this process. It is the means by which all the factors in a particular situation are considered – identifying the hazards, the potential degree and nature of any risk, and those possibly affected. The information gained from this assessment forms the basis of the ongoing planned management.

Risk management is a plan, strategy or programme that aims to manage the incident, event or hazard, removing those elements that would do harm, or reducing them to an acceptable level, and enabling any opportunity for positive gain to be taken as safely as possible. The situation is then closely monitored and periodically reviewed. For you, the primary aim is to protect people from harm, but there are secondary benefits of protecting a service or organisation from a loss of standards, safety or reputation, and of avoiding financial loss through compensation claims.

# 2  Regulatory context

Many regulations, policies and requirements surround the assessment and management of risk. The overarching legislation that concentrates on risk assessment and management is the *Health and Safety at Work etc Act 1974* and the *Management of Health and Safety at Work Regulations 1999* (Great Britain. Parliament 1974 and 1999) and their Northern Ireland counterparts (Great Britain. Parliament 1978 and 2000). Other legislation assumes an element of risk management in the actions that are required. Some of these pertain only to a particular field of practice, but many of the underlying principles are shared.

You should familiarise yourself with legislation that is relevant to your practice and your place and country of work. Legislation that is relevant to particular workplaces can be traced on the Health and Safety Executive website (*http://www.hse.gov.uk/legislation/trace*, 18.07.10), or the Health and Safety Executive for Northern Ireland (HSENI) website (*http://www.hseni.gov.uk/resources/legislation.htm*, 18.07.10).

If two sets of regulations both require risk to be assessed in the same given area, the assessment need only be done once, providing that the precautions taken meet the requirements of both sets of regulations.

All organisations should have their own local risk management procedures. You should familiarise yourself with these.

## 2.1 The Health and Safety at Work etc Act 1974

This Act (Great Britain. Parliament 1974) describes the general requirement for employers to ensure, as far as is reasonably practicable, the health, safety and welfare of their workforce and members of the public. This may be in terms of the environment, the materials or equipment used in the workplace, the demands of the work and the activities or actions of people in, or visiting, the workplace. Employers of more than five people must prepare a written health and safety policy and bring it to the attention of their employees. Employees are expected to co-operate with their employers and to take reasonable care for their own health and safety and that of others who may be affected by what they do, or do not do.

The Act (Great Britain. Parliament 1974) originally applied in England and Wales, Scotland (in part) and Northern Ireland (in part). Its requirements were redrawn for Northern Ireland with the *Health and Safety at Work (Northern Ireland) Order 1978* (Great Britain. Parliament 1978), which provides similar protection to employees in Northern Ireland.

The *Health and Safety at Work etc Act 1974* (Great Britain. Parliament 1974) created the Health and Safety Executive (HSE), the body responsible for the enforcement of workplace health and safety in England and Wales, and in Scotland in partnership with the Scottish Executive. Responsibility in Northern Ireland lies with the HSENI.

## 2.2 The Management of Health and Safety at Work Regulations 1999

The *Management of Health and Safety at Work Regulations 1999* (Great Britain. Parliament 1999), commonly termed the 'Management Regulations', require employers and the self-employed to assess the risks created by the hazards of their work. They must make arrangements for implementing the health and safety measures identified as necessary by risk assessments, appointing people with sufficient knowledge, skills, experience and training to help them to implement these arrangements. Employers must then monitor and review those arrangements.

Employees must be given clear information about any emergency procedures that might arise, along with any necessary supervision and training.

Employers must also work together with any other employer(s) operating from the same workplace, sharing information on the risks that other staff may be exposed to.

These regulations require employers to take particular account of risks to new and expectant mothers.

Those with five or more employees need to record the significant findings of a risk assessment – it is not necessary to record risk assessments for trivial or insignificant risks.

Although there is other more specific legislation for certain groups of people, situations or environments, the 'Management Regulations' (Great Britain. Parliament 1999) overlay all of these and require that *all* potential risks within the work setting are assessed and managed.

Residents of Northern Ireland should be aware of requirements laid down by the *Management of Health and Safety at Work Regulations (Northern Ireland) 2000* (Great Britain. Parliament 2000).

## 2.3 The Disability Discrimination Act 1995 and the Disability Discrimination Amendment Act 2005

The *Disability Discrimination Act 1995* (Great Britain. Parliament 1995a) is UK-wide legislation that brought in measures to prevent discrimination against disabled people. When you are working with colleagues or with service users, the fact that an individual has a disability does not necessarily mean that he or she signifies an additional risk to health and safety. As stated above, under the *Health and Safety at Work etc Act 1974* (Great Britain. Parliament 1974) employers must ensure, so far as is reasonably practicable, the health, safety and welfare of *all* their workforce.

The *Disability Discrimination Amendment Act 2005* (Great Britain. Parliament 2005a) builds on the previous legislation, so that employers must have due regard to their obligation to take disabled persons' disabilities into account and to make changes to the workplace where necessary, even where that involves treating disabled persons more favourably than other persons (Great Britain. Parliament 2005a, Part 5A, section 1(d)).

The risk assessment should identify the risks associated with the particular activity and should be specific to the individual carrying out a particular task, taking account of any reasonable adjustments put in place for the disabled person.

## 2.4 The Equality Act 2010

From 1 October 2010, the majority of the *Equality Act 2010* (Great Britain. Parliament 2010) replaces major parts of the provisions of the Disability Discrimination Act(s).

More information is available from:

• The Disability Rights Commission (DRC 2004), the Equality and Human Rights Commission website (*http://www.equalityhumanrights.com*, 18.07.10).

• The Government Equalities Office website (*http://www.equalities.gov.uk/equality_act_2010/equality_act_2010_what_do_i_n.aspx*, 18.07.10).

## 2.5 What is meant by 'reasonably practicable'?

An employer does not have to take measures to avoid or reduce the risk if it can be shown that it is technically impossible to do so or, if the time, the trouble or cost of the measures would be grossly disproportionate to the risk.

The HSE provides guidance on various terms used in health and safety legislation.

# 3 Risk assessment and management

There are five key steps to risk assessment and management, as shown in Figure 1. The figure also represents the continuous nature of the risk management process.

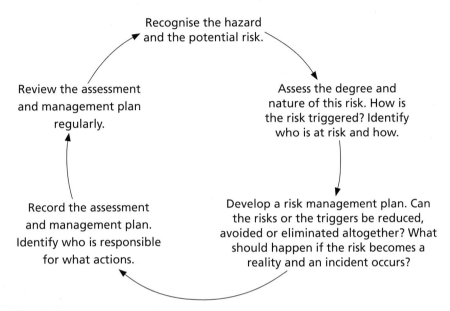

**Figure 1** The risk management process

## 3.1 Recognising the potential risk – risk assessment

A risk assessment is a structured method of identifying the hazards and the potential risks in any activity or situation. It needs to identify how the risk is triggered – are there any factors that make the risk more likely to occur? Are there warning signs, perhaps in the environment or in a person's behaviour, that indicate the potential risk might be about to happen? The assessment should also identify who may be affected by the risks and how.

McILwain (2006) suggests that risk assessment involves asking a series of questions that fall under the headings of 'identify', 'analyse' and 'control'. These may be shown as a grid, as follows:

| Identify | Analyse | Control |
|---|---|---|
| What could go wrong? | How often is this effect likely to occur? | How do you eliminate the risk/effect? |
| How could that happen? | How severe would be the effect? | How do you avoid the risk/effect? |
| What would be the effect? | What would be the cost of that effect? | How do you make the risk/effect less likely? |

**Figure 2** A risk assessment grid (taken from McIlwain 2006, p196 with permission of Radcliffe Publishing)

There are numerous tools for risk assessment, especially in areas such as falls prevention and manual handling. These tools can be useful to highlight or indicate possible hazards and for planning preventive action. However, information gathered from multiple sources needs to be put alongside clinical or professional judgement to give a comprehensive analysis of the potential risk. Where the situation involves service users, they, and all those involved in their care, need to be consulted. It is good practice, when a risk assessment concerns a particular service user, that you share your assessment with the individual (see section 3.5).

You need to be aware of any local policies or protocols that may exist for your organisation, as they may include preferred assessment tools or pro formas.

You will need to consider risk in each person's individual context. 'Risk is dynamic and may fluctuate – for example, a small task such as making a cup of tea may suddenly place an older person recovering from a broken hip at an increased risk of falling' (DH 2007b, section 1.5, p11).

### 3.1.1 Who is responsible?
In all cases, where the safety of employees, those who use their services and the public is concerned, it is the overall responsibility of employers or the self-employed to carry out the risk assessment. When the potential risk is to service users, through the work of an employee, the responsibility for carrying out the assessment may be devolved to the employee concerned. Whoever carries out the risk assessment should be appropriately trained to do so.

Although not responsible for carrying out risk assessments, trades union health and safety representatives are trained and accredited to participate in workplace inspections. They can also provide advice and information.

### 3.1.2 When to assess?
Risk assessment and management should be part of your everyday practice. You will be identifying possible hazards and risks as you observe, assess and work – as an individual, as part of a team or an organisation, or with your service users. Whether a specific risk assessment is carried out for a given activity/area of work depends upon the presence of hazards and the significance of any potential risk. You will need to consider what could occur, how and why it might happen, what the potential triggers or precursors to the risk occurring might be, when and how often it might happen and what the results could be. Assessment may confirm that adequate measures are already in place to eradicate or minimise the risk.

Formal risk assessments should be made before any significant changes are made to systems or practices, before any new project or activity is initiated, and before any particular actions or interventions are made that may engender risk. In these circumstances as much information as possible should be gathered to inform decision-making.

### 3.1.3 What risk?
'Risk assessment should be structured, evidence-based and as consistent as possible across settings and across service providers' (DH 2007a, p7). Consistency aids communication between practitioners and agencies, therefore improving care. The Department of Health document *Independence, choice and risk: a guide to best practice in supported decision making* (DH 2007b) aims to promote a common approach to risk

among all parties concerned in delivering care. Its guiding principle is applicable across the UK (see section 3.2).

Some hazards and risks are easy to identify: faulty electrical goods, uneven flooring or poor identification of care records. Other risks are more difficult to recognise, for example medication allergies, poor communication, or short-cuts in practice that might make something quicker or easier, but actually increase the potential for something to go wrong.

If you are trying to identify risks you need to consider how things happen in your work area. You need to use up-to-date, accurate information about how your service works, from both staff and service users, if possible. A collaborative approach will provide a fuller picture and a better understanding of the situation or circumstances that you are assessing.

Potential risks can be identified through data gathering and monitoring. Accident records, incident reports, sickness records and complaints can all highlight patterns of events or particular activities that are shown to be hazardous and potentially harmful. It is important that you routinely keep such information, as it will enable you or your organisation to identify risks at an early stage and to change your practice if necessary. Where you are making significant changes to existing systems or services, or if you are developing new projects, you will need to gather as much information as possible to inform your decision-making. Part of the risk assessment may need to include a literature/evidence search.

It is difficult to define how thorough or far-reaching risk assessments should be. When considering an occupational therapy service, you may need to consider risks arising from hazards related to:

• the physical working environment, including the use or provision of rehabilitation/ assistive equipment;

• the policies, procedures and/or practices of the organisation, the department and/or its personnel, including all therapeutic activity;

• the care plans for a service user or group of service users, considering their aims and priorities and influencing factors such as medication, recent events etc; and

• the actions, purposeful, accidental or unpredicted, of other people, including service users, their carers, other staff and members of the public.

### 3.1.4 Whose risk?
Having identified any hazards and the potential risk, you must then consider who or what is at risk of potential harm. Under the 'Management Regulations' (Great Britain. Parliament 1999), assessments should consider possible risk to all those affected by the work or activity. This may include service users, their families and carers, professional colleagues, other workers, students, volunteers and the public.

Some regulations do not specify that risks to the public should be assessed. However, considering the overarching requirement of the 'Management Regulations' (Great Britain. Parliament 1999), you still have to ensure that service users and/or members of the public are not adversely affected by any service activity.

## 3.2 Risk and choice

The Department of Health document *Independence, choice and risk: a guide to best practice in supported decision making* (DH 2007b), provides a governing principle behind good approaches to independence, choice and risk that is applicable across the UK. This is that:

*People have the right to live their lives to the full as long as that doesn't stop others from doing the same. To put this principle into practice, people supporting users of services have to:*

• *help people to have choice and control over their lives;*

• *recognise that making a choice can involve some risk;*

• *respect people's rights and those of their family and carers;*

• *help people understand their responsibilities and the implications of their choices, including any risks;*

• *acknowledge that there will always be some risk, and that trying to remove it altogether can outweigh the quality of life benefits for the person; and*

• *continue existing arrangements for safeguarding people.*

(Adapted from DH 2007b, pp12–13)

Mental capacity legislation (Great Britain. Parliament 2005b, Scotland. Scottish Executive 2000) states that although service users may make decisions that you may consider unwise or risky, it is not necessarily an indication that they lack capacity. In such a case your responsibility is to ensure that they are as safe as possible in their chosen circumstances.

## 3.3 Positive risk

Risk-taking is an integral component of good risk management. There is a growing amount of literature concerning positive or beneficial risk.

Positive risk-taking has been defined as:

*weighing up the potential benefits and harms of exercising one choice of action over another. This means identifying the potential risks involved, and developing plans and actions that reflect the positive potentials and stated priorities of the service user. It involves using available resources and support to achieve desired outcomes, and to minimise potential harmful outcomes.*

(Morgan 2004, p18)

*Positive risk management acknowledges that some degree of risk, or challenge, is essential to skill acquisition, self esteem and progress (College of Occupational Therapists 2006b). Positively managing risk does not mean being complacent about risk, but encourages a person-centred approach to evaluating it. Being risk averse can be seen as being part of the lack of hopefulness on the part of practitioners and a barrier to recovery (Deegan 2001, Perkins 2004).*

(Fieldhouse 2008, p501)

Morgan (2004) suggests a number of factors that enable positive risk-taking. Amongst these are:

• good supervision and organisational support;

• the development of appropriate management and intervention plans;

• working to realistic goals, broken down into shorter time frames;

• good communication; and

• clear lines of responsibility and accountability.

If you want to introduce safe and beneficial risk-taking, you may need to discuss this with your professional colleagues, using any evidence that is available to influence and change risk management plans, enabling service users to have more choice and become more engaged in activity.

## 3.4 Risk management

The assessment enables you to plan how risks are to be managed, what can reasonably and practicably be done or put in place to reduce the likelihood of the harmful risk occurring and how to increase the potential for a positive outcome. How can any warning signs or triggers be monitored and managed? What changes need to be made in systems and practices?

At the centre of this process should be a consideration of the service user's priorities, along with their personal skills and strengths that can be utilised as part of the management process. You need to use your professional reasoning and judgement to decide on the most appropriate action that will produce the desired outcomes. If the harmful risks cannot be eliminated or controlled to a reasonable level, the activity or situation should be amended or discontinued.

Risk management needs to be an organisational or 'whole system' approach, where everyone concerned understands and plays their part in managing the possible risk(s). This is an ongoing process that should enable you/your organisation to maintain a continuous reasonable level of safety, for yourself and those affected by your service.

### 3.4.1 What to do?
There are some obvious actions to take to manage harmful risk. First and foremost, you must follow the law. For example, hazardous chemicals must be stored securely according to the *Control of Substances Hazardous to Health Regulations 2002* (Great Britain. Parliament 2002). If local policies and procedures exist, such as fire precautions, then these must be followed. Some risks may be managed by reorganising work practices, work environments and/or providing protective equipment.

For less tangible risks, it is worth examining what causes the possible situation to arise. For example, violence and aggression, either verbal or physical, are a significant risk in some fields of work. Verbal aggression may be triggered for a number of reasons, including a perceived or real lack of information, a feeling of being rushed or of not being heard. Staff may reduce these possible precursors by adopting behaviours and communication styles that prevent anger or anxiety, or that can de-escalate situations should they occur. The introduction of communication skills training, alongside other strategies, could be the action taken to try to reduce the potential risk of violence and aggression in the workplace.

Appropriate training can be a significant factor in reducing and managing risk, although attendance at a training event does not necessarily ensure future safe working practice. The *Health and Safety at Work etc Act 1974* (Great Britain. Parliament 1974) states that employers must provide 'necessary information, instruction, training and supervision' (Great Britain. Parliament 1974, section 2, part 2). This encompasses training to prevent emergencies like fire, but also training that is relevant and necessary for any elements of a job that may entail risk, such as manual handling.

Section 13 of the *Management of Health and Safety at Work Regulations 1999* (Great Britain. Parliament 1999) similarly states that employers should provide health and safety training for their employees when they are recruited. Further training should be provided at any time when there is a change in the employee's responsibilities, the equipment used, the technology used or a change in systems of work.

The same regulations (Great Britain. Parliament 1999) also note that employers should take account of the capabilities of their employees when considering health and safety. This is encompassed in the College of Occupational Therapists' *Code of ethics and professional conduct* (COT 2010b), which states:

*You must only provide services and use techniques for which you are qualified by education, training and/or experience. These must be within your professional competence, appropriate to the needs of the service user and relate to your terms of employment.*

(College of Occupational Therapists 2010b, section 5.1, p27)

There are more general ongoing activities that can assist in the management or prevention of risk. Many of these are part of maintaining good standards of practice:

• Following evidence-based guidance and protocols can help you to keep your practice safe, enabling your (NHS) organisation to meet the National Health Services Litigation Authority (NHSLA) risk management standards and to benefit from reduced claims and risk management premiums. More information about the NHSLA risk management standards is available from its website (*http://www.nhsla.com/ RiskManagement*, 18.07.10).

• Observing good infection control practices, whether in a community, hospital or other setting.

• Keeping good therapy records, whether independently or as part of multidisciplinary notes, is vital in ensuring that you are providing appropriate, safe care.

• Continuing professional development can ensure that you are up to date with your knowledge and skills, and aware of best practice.

• Supervision and performance review systems allow ongoing monitoring of practice.

### 3.4.2 When to review?

Assessing and managing risk should be an ongoing process. It is vital to ensure that management plans and strategies are still relevant and that the risks originally identified are still adequately managed. A review should be done whenever a change occurs in the work or people involved which introduces significant new potential risks, if there has been an accident or incident, and/or at planned regular intervals.

## 3.5 Recording the assessment and its outcomes

It is good practice to record any risk assessments made related to the service, along with their outcomes, although this is a legal requirement only if the organisation has five or more employees. Written records can demonstrate that an organisation or service has complied with health and safety requirements. They can also provide a reminder to monitor certain areas of the service, if there are potential risks. Any risk assessment made in the course of providing an occupational therapy service to an individual must be recorded and a copy kept in the individual's care record.

Risk assessments may be recorded using a formal, purpose-designed risk assessment form, or they may be included as part of ongoing assessment and intervention notes. In whatever format, the records should show that a suitable and sufficient risk assessment was carried out and its outcomes recorded. You need to be able to show that 'a proper check was made; you asked who might be affected; you dealt with all the significant hazards, taking into account the number of people who could be involved; the precautions are reasonable, and the remaining risk is low; and you involved your staff or their representatives in the process' (HSE 2006b, p5).

The actions required to manage or control the risk(s) should be recorded along with the assessment information. This should detail what should be done, by whom and when. Any residual risk should also be detailed. The management plan or strategy should also consider what is to be done should an incident actually occur. A review date should be included as a prompt for future action.

The HSE has a number of example risk assessments for different settings that are available from its website (*http://www.hse.gov.uk/contact/faqs/riskassess.htm*, 18.07.10).

You should be familiar with the risk assessments and management plans present in your workplace(s).

It is good practice, when a risk assessment concerns a particular service user, to share your assessment with the individual. Where there are possible risks at an organisational level, for example in employment or working practices, it is good practice to pass on the results of your risk assessments and your management plans to your employer. This means that they are aware of the risks and your actions and may choose to monitor them or take appropriate action.

## 3.6 Integrated risk management

Risk management should be integrated into the work of an organisation, a service and your individual practice. For it to be done well, 'all parties need to work together, with a clarity of roles, opportunities for sharing information [and] seeking advice' (Bird and Dennis 2005).

There need to be systems for disseminating information and for ensuring that any required action is taken, for example if a National Patient Safety Agency patient safety alert is circulated which requires a change in practice, there must be a feedback system to communicate that the actions have been taken. Information management is important for facilitating access to, storage of and sharing of appropriate and correct information.

Service leads and managers have a role in ensuring that all their staff are aware of their risk management responsibilities and that they are familiar with local risk management procedures. All practitioners should be adequately skilled to fulfil these responsibilities. The more that you, as individuals and teams, are involved in your organisation's risk management activity, the better the general understanding will be of the potential hazards and risks across the organisation, and the more open communication, information sharing and learning will be, making systems simpler, with less duplication.

# 4   What happens if the risk becomes a reality?

It is not always possible to stop an incident from occurring, however well the potential risks have been managed or controlled. As stated, any risk management plan should also identify the action(s) required should an incident occur. Employing organisations are likely to have action plans for large, significant events which all employees should be familiar with.

Incidents or accidents can be better handled if you are well prepared. For example, when out of the workplace, you should always carry some means of communication plus useful contact numbers, or when accompanying a service user with a known condition that might need intervention, e.g. taking a snack for an insulin-dependent diabetic.

## 4.1 Managing a workplace incident or accident

If an incident or accident occurs, your priority is the safety of any people involved, whether staff, service users or public. First aid and other medical attention must be given and emergency services contacted if required. To ensure this happens, you should check that your organisation's arrangements for provision of first aid comply with legislative requirements. If there are any environmental hazards, evacuation procedures must be implemented. Again, the organisation and management need to ensure that staff know how to evacuate a building in an emergency, including moving service users if necessary.

If the incident involves an individual demonstrating dangerous or offensive behaviour, it may require the removal of that individual from the situation. Appropriately trained and authorised people will need to be involved. You must follow local policies and protocols.

Those involved in an incident or accident should be given the opportunity to talk about their experience and support should be provided where necessary.

## 4.2 Reporting an incident or accident

You must report any incidents that occur using your organisation's reporting mechanism. Some organisations also require the reporting of 'near misses', when an incident almost happens. This allows an organisation to evaluate the event, learn from it and change practice where required. Collecting and analysing service user comments and complaints also produces information that can be used to improve the quality of the service that you provide. Information services have an important role to play in risk management.

Under the *Reporting of Injuries, Diseases and Dangerous Occurrences Regulations 1995* (RIDDOR) (Great Britain. Parliament 1995b), employers, the self-employed and those in control of premises in England, Wales and Scotland must report specified workplace incidents to the HSE. These include deaths and major injuries, certain diseases, dangerous occurrences (near misses) and gas incidents. More information is available from the HSE.

A similar system exists with the HSENI, under the *Health and Safety at Work (Northern Ireland) Order 1978* (Great Britain. Parliament 1978) and the *Reporting of Injuries, Diseases and Dangerous Occurrences Regulations (Northern Ireland) 1997* (Great Britain. Parliament 1997).

Should an incident occur involving a service user, it is vital that you enter a full record of the event in their care records, along with a record of any follow-up action taken. You should record recommendations for any changes to practice to prevent or manage future risk. Further information on record-keeping issues is available in the College of Occupational Therapists' 2010 guidance document *Record keeping* (COT 2010d).

The National Patient Safety Agency (NPSA) was set up to improve safety and quality of care through reporting, analysing and learning from adverse incidents and near misses across the UK health service. Its National Reporting and Learning System is an electronic database that facilitates the reporting of service user safety incidents, including the near misses. From this collated information the NPSA can distribute guidance or initiate preventative measures, so the benefits are gained across the country.

Further information is available from the NPSA website (*http://www.npsa.nhs.uk/*, 18.07.10).

The Medicines and Healthcare products Regulatory Agency (MHRA) ensures that medicines and medical devices work and are acceptably safe to use. It will monitor the safety of medicines and devices, approving them for use and providing advice or warnings to users. The MHRA ensures that manufacturers adhere to regulations, providing a certificate or licence before the product is released for general use.

Further information is available from the MHRA website (*http://www.mhra.gov.uk/*, 18.07.10).

# 5 Further information and resources

## 5.1 Community and social care

The move towards personalisation and the transformation of community equipment services may mean an increased focus on risk assessment and risk management by services in relation to individual service users (see sections 3.2 and 3.3).

Social Care Online (*http://www.scie-socialcareonline.org.uk/search.asp*, 18.07.10) is a useful knowledge database hosted by the Social Care Institute for Excellence. It is a large resource of information related to community and social care, including risk. Some documents are available for immediate download; other journal articles require payment to access.

## 5.2 Employment and recruitment

Concerns have been raised around risks associated with reduced staffing levels and the pressure of meeting targets and standards in service provision. Your priority in these circumstances is to ensure service user safety. Practitioners and service leads need to discuss their concerns with their management team and ask for guidance. Management should be informed that statutory targets and standards may not be met and the reasons why. If concerns are high within your service or department, a risk assessment should be carried out to support any discussion with your organisation.

Service leads may need to think in terms of organisational risks associated with downsizing, 'down banding' or delegating to lower grade staff and how such risks may be managed as far as possible. Organisational managers need to be made aware of such risks and of the approach being taken to minimise them. For example:

- Low morale and high stress levels can lead to poor practice and 'cutting corners', raising the likelihood of an incident occurring that may harm a service user or practitioner. Service leads need to ensure adequate training, monitoring and support for staff to minimise the risk of things going wrong.

- Supervision must be adequate to identify and manage poor or inadequate performance.

- Practitioners must be aware of and maintain good lone working practice if relevant.

- You must prioritise record keeping. A heavy workload is not acceptable as an excuse for inadequate records if litigation occurs.

The Royal College of Nursing has also highlighted the risks associated with low staffing (RCN 2010).

When working with children and young people, practitioners must be aware of the requirements generated by the *Safeguarding Vulnerable Groups Act 2006* (Great Britain. Parliament 2006) and the Scottish equivalent, *Protection of Vulnerable Groups (Scotland) Act 2007* (Scotland. Scottish Executive 2007).

## 5.3 Equipment and adaptations

You may use, and also teach service users, carers or colleagues to use, a wide range of equipment and adaptations. It is important to familiarise yourself with any national or local policies or guidance in the use or maintenance of equipment, especially in those areas where a detailed risk assessment may be required, for example use of bed rails or equipment for obese service users.

The Medicines and Healthcare products Regulatory Agency (MHRA) produces a range of resources that may be helpful to you, all of which are available on its website (*http://www.mhra.gov.uk/index.htm*, 18.07.10).

A specific section of the website has been adapted to meet the needs of occupational therapists and includes access to interactive education modules:

- *http://www.mhra.gov.uk/Safetyinformation/Healthcareproviders/
  Physiotherapyandoccupationaltherapy/index.htm*                Accessed on 18.07.10.

Other useful publications from the MHRA include:

- *Medicines and medical devices regulations – what you need to know* (2008)

- *Faulty medical equipment – how do I report it?* (undated)

- *Managing medical devices: Guidance for healthcare and social services organisations* (2006)

For further information about the provision of equipment and adaptations by local authorities and NHS boards in Scotland see *Guidance on the provision of equipment and adaptations* (Scottish Government et al 2009), which has been endorsed by the College of Occupational Therapists. A specific section relates to health and safety responsibilities and risk. It is available to download from: *http://www.sehd.scot.nhs.uk/publications/CC2009_05.pdf*, 18.07.10.

## 5.4 Lone working/personal safety

Working alone does not automatically imply being more at risk, but it is worth considering any additional systems or processes required to ensure safe working, and the actions necessary to manage an incident should it occur.

If you are working off-site or in non-clinical areas, you may be around other workers, but they may not work for the same organisation or to the same incident management procedures. When any service is set up in such circumstances, an agreed system must be put in place where there is an assured response to an alarm call.

The following are all guides on lone working written by various organisations:

- Health and Safety Executive (2009a) *Working alone. Health and safety guidance on the risks of working alone.* London: HSE. Available from: *http://www.hse.gov.uk/pubns/indg73.pdf*                Accessed on 18.07.10.

- NHS Security Management Service (2009) *Developing a policy for the protection of lone workers.* 2nd ed. London: NHS Counter Fraud and Security Management Service. Available from: *http://www.nhsbsa.nhs.uk/Documents/SecurityManagement/Lone_Working_policy_template.pdf*                Accessed on 18.07.10.

- NHS Security Management Service (2005) *Not alone: A guide for the better protection of lone workers in the NHS*. London: NHS Counter Fraud and Security Management Service. Available from: *http://www.nhsbsa.nhs.uk/SecurityManagement/Documents/ not_alone.pdf*                                                      Accessed on 18.07.10.

- Partnership for Occupational Safety and Health in Healthcare, NHS Security Management Service (2009) *Improving safety for lone workers. A guide for managers*. London: NHS Employers. Available from: *http://www.nhsemployers.org/ SiteCollectionDocuments/Improving%20safety%20for%20lone%20workers%20-%20 managers%20guide%20FINAL.pdf*                                    Accessed on 18.07.10.

- UNISON also has a number of guides on different elements of safe lone working practice available through its searchable documents database: *http://www.unison.org. uk/resources/docs_list.asp*                                       Accessed on 18.07.10.

- The Suzy Lamplugh Trust has a growing resource of guides on personal safety. Further information is available on its website: *http://www.suzylamplugh.org/personalsafety/ personal-safety-tips*                                           Accessed on 18.07.10.

# 5.5 Mental health

There are numerous resources concerning risk management in the mental health setting, especially in the benefits of positive risk.

The College of Occupational Therapists has prepared a briefing on *Mental health and care co-ordination* (COT 2010c) that provides information about the Care Programme Approach, the role and core competencies of the care coordinator, which is often an occupational therapist. It also considers the role in relation to risk management and medicines management.

*Best practice in managing risk: principles and evidence for best practice in the assessment and management of risk to self and others in mental health services* (DH 2007a) provides best practice points for effective risk management, stressing the importance of basing decisions on the best evidence, information and clinical judgement available, putting the service user at the centre, the benefits of positive risk, collaboration, and organisational strategy.

*Living with risk. Mental health service users and their involvement in risk assessment and management* (Langan and Lindow 2004) is an exploration of risk assessment and risk management for people being discharged from psychiatric hospital into the community.

The Sainsbury Centre for Mental Health (now The Centre for Mental Health) produced a practical tool for risk assessment and management in mental health services. *Clinical risk management. A clinical tool and practitioner manual* (2000) looks at the potential risks of suicide, self-neglect and violence/aggression and at the support networks available. The pack includes a template of the tool, a practitioner guide, and case studies exploring the issues that might be encountered in the field. It is available to download free from: *http://www.centreformentalhealth.org.uk/publications/clinical_risk_ management.aspx*, 18.07.10.

*A guide to risk management in mental health* (O'Rourke and Bird 2001) gives the basic principles of risk assessment, the duty of care and the importance of learning the lessons from public inquiries, while also offering practical guidance for implementing risk management in mental health services. It shows how effective risk assessment and management can be empowering for mental health service users.

Other publications that may be useful include:

- NHS Litigation Authority (2010) *NHSLA mental health and learning disability standards – 2010/11*. London: NHSLA. Available to download from: *http://www.nhsla.com/ RiskManagement*                                                                          Accessed on 18.07.10.

- Petch E (2001) Risk management in UK mental health services – an overvalued idea? *Psychiatric Bulletin*, 25(6), 203–205.

- Royal College of Psychiatrists (2008) *Rethinking risk to others in mental health services: final report of a scoping group* (College Report CR150). London: Royal College of Psychiatrists. Available at: *http://www.rcpsych.ac.uk/files/pdfversion/CR150.pdf*
Accessed on 18.07.10.

## 5.6 Research

'Research can involve an element of risk, both in terms of return on investment and sometimes for the safety and well-being of the research participant' (DH 2005a, p2).

Research governance aims to 'improve the quality of research, and provide safeguards for the public by:

- enhancing ethical and scientific quality,

- promoting good practice,

- reducing adverse incidents and ensuring lessons are learnt and

- forestalling poor performance and misconduct'. (DH 2005a, p1)

Each of the four UK countries has a research governance framework which is similar in purpose and content.

The UK Research Integrity Office's *Code of practice for research* (UKRIO 2009) has been designed to encourage good conduct in research and help prevent misconduct, in order to assist organisations and researchers to conduct research of the highest quality. It provides general principles and standards for good practice in research, applicable to both individual researchers and organisations that carry out, fund, host or are otherwise involved in research. A one-page 'recommended checklist for researchers' can be found on the inside of the front cover. This is a non-technical checklist summarising the key points of good practice in research and is applicable to all subject areas. The checklist is based on the more detailed standards given in section 3. It suggests that the risk assessment should determine:

- *whether there are any ethical issues and whether ethics review is required;*

- *the potential for risks to the organisation, the research, or the health, safety and wellbeing of researchers and research participants; and*

- *what legal requirements govern the research.*

(UKRIO 2009)

*The safety of participants and of research and other staff must be given priority at all times, and health and safety regulations must be strictly observed.*

(DH 2005a, p14)

The Department of Health research governance risk assessment tool (DH 2005b pp30–33) identifies further key risk areas in relation to subject/participant characteristics, researcher competence, the nature of the information being sought, appropriateness of methodology to subject and quality of research design, methods/nature of data collection, level of privacy to participant, relationship between investigator and participants, and external considerations.

Risks must be in proportion to the potential benefit of the research and explained clearly to the research participant.

It is essential that as a researcher, you conduct a risk assessment as part of the development of your research proposal. If there are potential risks, you must identify how those risks will be minimised. Application forms for ethical approval will require you to provide details about assessed risks and their management.

Commissioners of health and social care are increasingly looking for services that can demonstrate they are cost effective and evidence based. Occupational therapy services are potentially at risk if they fail to collect comprehensive evidence of the effectiveness of occupational therapy interventions. Therefore, you need to support and actively engage in evidence-based practice and research-related activities.

The following resources provide further information relating to research governance:

- College of Occupational Therapists (2010a) *Applying for ethics approval for research* (COT/BAOT Briefings 82). London: COT.

- Department of Health (2005a) *Research governance framework for health and social care*. 2nd ed. London: DH.

- Department of Health (2005b) *Research governance framework resource pack*. London: DH.

- Department of Health, Social Services and Public Safety (2006) *Research governance framework for health and social care*. 2nd ed. Belfast: DHSSPS.

- Scottish Executive Health Department (2006) *Research governance framework for health and community care*. 2nd ed. Edinburgh: SEHD.

- UK Research Integrity Office (2009) *Code of practice for research. Promoting good practice and preventing misconduct*. London: UKRIO.

- Wales Office of Research and Development for Health and Social Care (2009) *Research governance framework for health and social care in Wales*. 2nd ed. Cardiff: WORD.

## 5.7 Work-related violence

The HSE defines work-related violence as: 'Any incident in which a person is abused, threatened or assaulted in circumstances relating to their work' (Health and Safety Executive 2004, p1).

The Government's acceptance of the recommendations of the 2001 *National task force on violence against social care staff* led to a £2m campaign to reduce violence in England. The DH website has reports and resources to enable employers to minimise the potential for their staff to be subject to violence and abuse (*http://www.dh.gov.uk/en/Publicationsandstatistics/Publications/PublicationsPolicyAndGuidance/DH_4010625*, 27.10.10).

There are a number of guides from the HSE and other organisations which may be helpful to you:

- Health and Safety Executive, Health Services Advisory Committee (1997) *Violence and aggression to staff in health services – guidance on assessment and management.* London: HSE Books.

- Health and Safety Executive (2000) Local authority circular. *Work related violence.* (LAC 88/2). London: HSE.

- Health and Safety Executive (2004) *Violence at work. A guide for employers.* London: HSE.

- Advisory, Conciliation and Arbitration Service; Department for Business, Innovation and Skills; Confederation of British Industry; Health and Safety Executive et al (2010) *Preventing workplace harassment and violence: joint guidance implementing a European social partner agreement.* London: ACAS; BIS; CBI; HSE; PPE; TUC. Available at: *http://www.workplaceharassment.org.uk/wp-content/uploads/2009/11/HRE_100_Guidance_report.pdf*                    Accessed on 23.07.10.

- UNISON (undated) *Violence at work. A guide to risk prevention.* London: UNISON.

- National task force on violence against social care staff website: *http://www.dh.gov.uk/en/Publicationsandstatistics/Publications/PublicationsPolicyAndGuidance/DH_4010625*                    Accessed on 27.10.10.

## 5.8 General information

You should seek advice and assistance from your local clinical governance, health and safety, risk management, quality and/or research departments.

- Dimond B (2004) *Legal aspects of occupational therapy.* 2nd ed. London: Blackwell Publishing.

- Lynch J (2009) *Health records in court.* Oxford: Radcliffe Publishing.

- Health and Safety Executive
  Britain's HSE is responsible for the regulation of almost all the risks to health and safety arising from work activity in Britain. Further information is available on its website: *http://www.hse.gov.uk/*, 18.07.10. The following are HSE publications, available from its website:

  ⊃ Health and Safety Executive (1997) *Successful health and safety management.* London: HSE.

  ⊃ Health and Safety Executive (1999) *Reducing error and influencing behaviour.* London: HSE.

  ⊃ Health and Safety Executive (2006a) *Essentials of health and safety at work.* 4th ed. London: HSE.

  ⊃ Health and Safety Executive (2006b) *Five steps to risk assessment.* London: HSE.

➲ Health and Safety Executive (2008) *Health and safety regulation – a short guide.* London: HSE.

➲ Health and Safety Executive (2009b) *Health and safety for disabled workers and those who work with them: an easy read guide.* London: HSE.

• Health and Safety Executive for Northern Ireland
HSENI is the lead body responsible for the promotion and enforcement of health and safety at work standards in Northern Ireland. Further information is available on its website: *http://www.hseni.gov.uk/*, 18.07.10.

• Health and Safety Executive Scotland
Workplace health and safety legislation is still overseen by the UK Parliament. The power to make or change health and safety legislation has not been devolved. The HSE works closely with the Scottish Executive. Further information is available on its website: *http://www.hse.gov.uk/scotland/index.htm*, 18.07.10.

• National Health Service Litigation Authority
The NHSLA handles negligence claims and works to improve risk management practices in the NHS in England. Further information is available on its website: *http://www.nhsla.com/home.htm*, 18.07.10.

• Regulatory bodies
There are a number of bodies across the UK that regulate health and social care:

➲ The Care Quality Commission is the independent regulator of health and social care in England. It regulates care provided by the NHS, local authorities, private companies and voluntary organisations. Further information is available on its website: *http://www.cqc.org.uk/*, 18.07.10.

➲ The Care and Social Services Standards Inspectorate for Wales regulates social care, early years and social services in Wales. *http://wales.gov.uk/cssiwsubsite/ newcssiw/?lang=en*, 18.07.10.

➲ The Healthcare Inspectorate Wales is the independent inspectorate and regulator of all healthcare in Wales. *http://www.hiw.org.uk/*, 18.07.10.

➲ The Scottish Commission for the Regulation of Care regulates all adult, child and independent healthcare services in Scotland. *http://www.carecommission.com*, 18.07.10.

➲ The Regulation and Quality Improvement Authority registers and inspects a wide range of health and social care services in Northern Ireland. *http://www.rqia.org.uk/ home/index.cfm*, 18.07.10.

Advisory, Conciliation and Arbitration Service; Department for Business, Innovation and Skills; Confederation of British Industry et al (2010) *Preventing workplace harassment and violence: joint guidance implementing a European social partner agreement.* London: ACAS; BIS; CBI; HSE; PPE; TUC.

Available at: *http://www.workplaceharassment.org.uk/wpcontent/uploads/2009/11/ HRE_100_Guidance_report.pdf* Accessed on 23.07.10.

Barry M (2007) *Effective approaches to risk assessment in social work: an international literature review.* Edinburgh: Scottish Executive.

Bird D, Dennis S (2005) Integrating risk management into working practice. *Nursing Standard, 20(13),* 52–54.

Care and Social Services Standards Inspectorate for Wales website:
*http://wales.gov.uk/cssiwsubsite/newcssiw/?lang=en* Accessed on 18.07.10.

Care Quality Commission (CQC) website:
*http://www.cqc.org.uk/* Accessed on 18.07.10.

College of Occupational Therapists (2006a) *Manual handling.* (Guidance 3). London: COT.

College of Occupational Therapists (2006b) *Recovering ordinary lives: the strategy for occupational therapy services 2007–2017: a vision for the next ten years.* London: COT, cited in Fieldhouse J (2008) Community mental health. In: J Creek, L Lougher, eds. *Occupational therapy and mental health.* 4th ed. Edinburgh: Churchill Livingstone.

College of Occupational Therapists (2010a) *Applying for ethics approval for research* (COT/BAOT Briefing 82). London: COT.

College of Occupational Therapists (2010b) *Code of ethics and professional conduct.* London: COT.

College of Occupational Therapists (2010c) *Mental health care co-ordination.* (COT/ BAOT Briefing). London: COT [in press].

College of Occupational Therapists (2010d) *Record keeping.* 2nd ed. London: COT.

Deegan PE (2001) Recovery as a self-directed process of healing and transformation. *Occupational Therapy in Mental Health, 17(1),* 5–21, cited in Fieldhouse J (2008) Community mental health. In: J Creek, L Lougher, eds. *Occupational therapy and mental health.* 4th ed. Edinburgh: Churchill Livingstone.

Department of Health (2005a) *Research governance framework for health and social care.* 2nd ed. London: DH.

Department of Health (2005b) *Research governance framework resource pack.* London: DH.

Department of Health (2007a) *Best practice in managing risk: principles and evidence for best practice in the assessment and management of risk to self and others in mental health services.* London: DH.

Department of Health (2007b) *Independence, choice and risk: a guide to best practice in supported decision making.* London: DH.

Department of Health, Social Services and Public Safety (2006) *Research governance framework for health and social care.* 2nd ed. Belfast: DHSSPS.

Dimond B (2004) *Legal aspects of occupational therapy.* 2nd ed. London: Blackwell Publishing.

Disability Rights Commission (2004) *Disability Discrimination Act 1995: code of practice: employment and occupation.* London: Stationery Office.

Fieldhouse J (2008) Community mental health. In: J Creek, L Lougher, eds. *Occupational therapy and mental health.* 4th ed. Edinburgh: Churchill Livingstone.

Great Britain. Parliament (1974) *Health and Safety at Work etc Act 1974.* London: HMSO.

Great Britain. Parliament (1978) *Health and Safety at Work (Northern Ireland) Order 1978.* (No.1039 (NI 9)). London: HMSO.

Great Britain. Parliament (1995a) *Disability Discrimination Act 1995.* London: HMSO.

Great Britain. Parliament (1995b) *Reporting of Injuries, Diseases and Dangerous Occurrences Regulations 1995.* London: HMSO.

Great Britain. Parliament (1997) *Reporting of Injuries, Diseases and Dangerous Occurrences Regulations (Northern Ireland) 1997.* (Statutory Rule 1997 No. 455). London: HMSO.

Great Britain. Parliament (1999) *Management of Health and Safety at Work Regulations 1999.* (SI 1999 No. 3242). London: Stationery Office.

Great Britain. Parliament (2000) *Management of Health and Safety at Work Regulations (Northern Ireland) 2000.* (Statutory Rule 2000 No. 388). London: Stationery Office.

Great Britain. Parliament (2002) *Control of Substances Hazardous to Health Regulations 2002.* London: Stationery Office.

Great Britain. Parliament (2005a) *Disability Discrimination Amendment Act 2005.* London: Stationery Office.

Great Britain. Parliament (2005b) *Mental Capacity Act 2005.* London: Stationery Office.

Great Britain. Parliament (2006) *Safeguarding Vulnerable Groups Act 2006.* London: Stationery Office.

Great Britain. Parliament (2010) *Equality Act 2010.* London: Stationery Office.

Health and Safety Executive (1997) *Successful health and safety management.* London: HSE.

Health and Safety Executive (1999) *Reducing error and influencing behaviour.* London: HSE.

Health and Safety Executive (2000) *Local authority circular. Work related violence. (LAC 88/2).* London: HSE.

Health and Safety Executive (2004) *Violence at work. A guide for employers.* London: HSE.

Health and Safety Executive (2006a) *Essentials of health and safety at work.* 4th ed. London: HSE.

Health and Safety Executive (2006b) *Five steps to risk assessment.* London: HSE.

Health and Safety Executive (2008) *Health and safety regulation – a short guide.* London: HSE.

Health and Safety Executive (2009a) *Working alone. Health and safety guidance on the risks of working alone.* London: HSE.
Available from: *http://www.hse.gov.uk/pubns/indg73.pdf*          Accessed on 18.07.10.

Health and Safety Executive (2009b) *Health and safety for disabled workers and those who work with them: an easy read guide.* London: HSE.

Health and Safety Executive website:
*http://www.hse.gov.uk/*                                        Accessed on 18.07.10.

Health and Safety Executive, Health Services Advisory Committee (1997) *Violence and aggression to staff in health services – guidance on assessment and management.* London: HSE Books.

Health and Safety Executive for Northern Ireland (HSENI) website: *http://www.hseni.gov. uk/*
                                                                 Accessed on 18.07.10.

Health and Safety Executive Scotland website: *http://www.hse.gov.uk/scotland/index. htm*
                                                                 Accessed on 18.07.10.

Healthcare Inspectorate Wales website:
*http://www.hiw.org.uk/*                                         Accessed on 18.07.10.

Langan J, Lindow V (2004) *Living with risk. Mental health service users and their involvement in risk assessment and management.* Bristol: The Policy Press.

Lynch J (2009) *Health records in court.* Oxford: Radcliffe Publishing.

McILwain JC (2006) A review: a decade of clinical risk management and risk tools. *Clinician in Management, 14(4),* 189–199.

Medicines and Healthcare products Regulatory Agency (2006) *Managing medical devices: Guidance for healthcare and social services organisations*. DB2006(05). London: MHRA.

Medicines and Healthcare products Regulatory Agency (2008) *Medicines and medical devices regulations – what you need to know.* London: MHRA.

Medicines and Healthcare products Regulatory Agency (undated) *Faulty medical equipment – how do I report it?* London: MHRA.

Medicines and Healthcare products Regulatory Agency (MHRA) website: *http://www.mhra.gov.uk/*                    Accessed on 18.07.10.

Morgan S (2000) *Clinical risk management. A clinical tool and practitioner manual.* London: Sainsbury Centre for Mental Health. Available from: *http://www. centreformentalhealth.org.uk/publications/clinical_risk_management.aspx*
                                          Accessed on 18.07.10.

Morgan S (2004) Positive risk taking: an idea whose time has come. *Health Care Risk Report, 10(10),* 18–19.

National Health Service Litigation Authority website: *http://www.nhsla.com/home.htm*                    Accessed on 18.07.10.

National Patient Safety Agency website: *http://www.npsa.nhs.uk/*                    Accessed on 18.07.10.

NHS Litigation Authority (2010) *NHSLA mental health and learning disability standards – 2010/11.* London: NHSLA.
Available from: *http://www.nhsla.com/RiskManagement/*          Accessed on 18.07.10.

NHS Litigation Authority [ca. 2010] *Risk management: NHSLA standards and assessments.* London: NHS Litigation Authority.
Available at: http://www.nhsla.com/RiskManagement/          Accessed on 18.07.10

NHS Security Management Service (2005) *Not alone: A guide for the better protection of lone workers in the NHS.* London: NHS Counter Fraud and Security Management Service.
Available from: *http://www.nhsbsa.nhs.uk/SecurityManagement/Documents/not_alone. pdf*                    Accessed on 18.07.10.

NHS Security Management Service (2009) *Developing a policy for the protection of lone workers.* 2nd ed. London: NHS Counter Fraud and Security Management Service.
Available from: *http://www.nhsbsa.nhs.uk/Documents/SecurityManagement/Lone_ Working_policy_template.pdf*                    Accessed on 18.07.10.

O'Rourke M, Bird L (2001) *A guide to risk management in mental health*. London: Mental Health Foundation.

Partnership for Occupational Safety and Health in Healthcare, NHS Security Management Service (2009) *Improving safety for lone workers. A guide for managers.* London: NHS Employers.

Available from: *http://www.nhsemployers.org/SiteCollectionDocuments/Improving%20 safety%20for%20lone%20workers%20-%20managers%20guide%20FINAL.pdf*
Accessed on 18.07.10.

Perkins RE (2004) *Recovery and rehabilitation.* Paper presented at the Avon and Wiltshire Mental Health Partnership Annual Rehabilitation Service Conference. 23 January 2004, Vassal Centre, Bristol, cited in Fieldhouse J (2008) Community mental health. In: J Creek, L Lougher, eds. *Occupational therapy and mental health.* 4th ed. Edinburgh: Churchill Livingstone.

Petch E (2001) Risk management in UK mental health services – an overvalued idea? *Psychiatric Bulletin, 25(6),* 203–205.

Regulation and Quality Improvement Authority website:
*http://www.rqia.org.uk/home/index.cfm*                    Accessed on 18.07.10.

Royal College of Nursing (2010) *Public unaware of scale of NHS cutbacks.* London: RCN. Available at: *http://www.rcn.org.uk/newsevents/news/article/uk/public_unaware_of_ scale_of_nhs_cutbacks*                    Accessed on 18.07.10.

Royal College of Psychiatrists (2008) *Rethinking risk to others in mental health services: final report of a scoping group.* (College Report CR150). London: Royal College of Psychiatrists.
Available at: http://www.rcpsych.ac.uk/files/pdfversion/CR150.pdf   Accessed on 18.07.10.

Scotland. Scottish Executive (2000) *Adults with Incapacity (Scotland) Act 2000.* Edinburgh: Stationery Office.

Scotland. Scottish Government (2007) *Protection of Vulnerable Groups (Scotland) Act 2007 (asp 14).* Edinburgh: Scottish Government. Available at: *http://www.opsi.gov.uk/ legislation/scotland/acts2007/asp_20070014_en_1*                    Accessed on 20.07.10.

Scottish Commission for the Regulation of Care (SCRCS) website:
*http://www.carecommission.com*                    Accessed on 18.07.10.

Scottish Executive Health Department (2006) *Research Governance Framework for Health and Community Care.* 2nd ed. Edinburgh: SEHD.

Scottish Government, College of Occupational Therapists, COSLA (2009) *Guidance on the provision of equipment and adaptations.* Edinburgh: Scottish Government. Available from: *http://www.sehd.scot.nhs.uk/publications/CC2009_05.pdf*
Accessed on 18.07.10.

Social Care Online
http://www.scie-socialcareonline.org.uk/search.asp                    Accessed on 18.07.10.

Suzy Lamplugh Trust website:
*http://www.suzylamplugh.org/personal-safety/personal-safety-tips/*
Accessed on 18.07.10.

UK Research Integrity Office (2009) *Code of practice for research: promoting good practice and preventing misconduct.* London: UKRIO.

UNISON website:

*http://www.unison.org.uk/resources/docs_list.asp*                    Accessed on 18.07.10.

UNISON (undated) *Violence at work. A guide to risk prevention.* London: UNISON.

Wales Office of Research and Development for Health and Social Care (2009) *Research governance framework for health and social care in Wales.* 2nd ed. Cardiff: WORD.

# Bibliography

Department of Health; Social Care, Local Government and Care Partnerships (SCLGCP) Directorate; Older People and Dementia (2010) *Nothing ventured, nothing gained: risk guidance for people with dementia.* London: DH.

Dimond BC (2004) *Legal aspects of occupational therapy.* 2nd ed. Oxford: Blackwell Science.

Health and Safety Executive (2004) *Violence at work: a guide for employers.* London: HSE.

Health and Safety Executive (2005*) Working alone in safety: controlling the risks of solitary work.* London: HSE.

NHS Scotland (2007) Clinical governance: educational resources. Edinburgh: NHS Quality Improvement Scotland, Clinical Governance Support and Development Unit. Available at: *http://www.clinicalgovernance.scot.nhs.uk/section3/identifyrisk.asp*
Accessed on 18.07.10.

Occupational Therapy Benchmarking Group (2001) *Benchmark statement: health care programmes: phase 1: occupational therapy.* Gloucester: Quality Assurance Agency for Higher Education.

Petch E (2001) Risk management in UK mental health services: an overvalued idea? *Psychiatric Bulletin, 25(6),* 203–205.

Social Care Online [database] *http://www.scie-socialcareonline.org.uk/search.asp*
Accessed on 18.07.10.